Raising
Five
Daughters

The Estrogen Conspiracy

A Father's Positive Way
To Look at the Spiritual
And Emotional Needs Involved in
Raising Daughters

Rick Harrison

Introduction

A s a way to introduce myself, let me begin by saying I am a very blessed man. I live with five beautiful and wonderful daughters and one very understanding wife. My journey into father-hood began a mere 17 years ago with the birth of our first daughter and hopefully has concluded with the birth of our last two, who are both now 7 years old. I have to openly admit that I am still as confused now as in the beginning as to why God gave me all of these women.

I am now a pastor, but I began my adult profes-sional career as a high school teacher and football coach. Even though well versed in the abilities to motivate young men on the field of athletic competition, I still struggle with exactly what formula works when it comes to motivating young girls on their journeys to womanhood. Admittedly, this book is not a conclusive text on the exact way to raise your daughter or daughters. It is more a reflection of some hilarious experiences and some humbling moments from the life of one father.

Let me further add in this introduction just how this all came to be. After we had been married for about three years, my wife and I began to plan for children. Six years later and a lot of help from some special fertility doctors, our first child, Jessica, arrived. It was at this point that we purposed to allow God to bless us with the number of children He saw fit. About 17 months later our second daughter, Mikayla, came along, and I was convinced God must be finished with our quiver.

A few years later while doing some mission work with our denomination's mission board a long way from our home state of Oklahoma, my wife needed some medical tests. The doctor's recommendation was to pursue pregnancy, and although hesitant at first I slowly became increasingly excited that this might be another opportunity for a male child. Daughter number three, Lydia, was born in Indiana, and before we could complete the moving process back to Oklahoma, Dayna became pregnant again, and I just knew—male child! Shortly after the move Dayna miscarried for the second time; it was a difficult experience as many who read this will be able to relate. However, we settled into our new ministry in Oklahoma with things cruising along well. A few days before Christmas 2003, (I was 42; Dayna was 40.) Dayna came home with some news from what I thought was an annual check-up. Instead she showed up with an ultrasound picture; by this time I was very familiar with looking at these. I missed something when I looked though. Dayna insisted I look again, and sure enough she was right; there were two. I immediately thought yes, God, a 50/50 chance at a male child! Nope! That was God's answer. Samantha and Emma were born in August.

So now Dayna and I have five daughters, beautiful, healthy works in progress.

As you will see in the pages of this book, I've come to the conclusion that I may be the work in progress much more so than my children. My prayer in writing this is to help all those men out there to see they can have just as much fun with those little girls with whom God has blessed them and also to express just a few of the things I've learned along the journey thus far. They are delicate creatures, my daughters, and it is important that as a father I always keep this in mind. The final thing I want to add as a way of introduction is this: Have fun! A sense of humor goes a long way in learning to be the parent God intends for us to be.

Chapter 1

". . . instead bring them up in the training
and instruction of the Lord"
Ephesians 6:4

What a daunting task it is as parents to raise our children in such a way that when grown, they will have the proper perspective of Who God is and what He desires from each of them! Desiring to see our children grow in the Lord, Dayna and I have always prayed that our own spiritual growth along with our training of them would take hold. I never had a better demonstration than one spring day while we were serving in Indiana.

While serving as pastor of a new church plant in Indiana, I had become increasingly busy with all the "stuff" that demands one's time when undertaking such a project. Dayna had pointed out that I needed to slow down and dedicate a bit more time with my daughters; Jessica was six at the time and Mikayla was four. I realized she was having one of those female intuitive moments and listened—something I've learned to do as we've been married 26 years as of this writing.

I love the outdoors and had heard from some people around the area that there was an excellent place to fish along the banks of a local reservoir. I asked Jessica if she would like to go fishing with daddy. Without hesitation she said that would be great. The next morning, we got everything together and left just after lunch. Having arrived at the parking location, we unloaded the truck. Jessica had her rod, and I had the rest of the load: tackle box, my rod and reel, backpack with food and drinks, and bait. I looked like a pack mule, and Jessica was traveling light.

We walked down a long path through old-growth timber—the kind of trees that have a canopy effect. As we hiked in, we paused and just took in the beauty of God's creation. When we arrived at the lake shore, we were greeted by large rock ledges and pristine water in a cove that we had all to ourselves. We quickly unloaded and readied ourselves to fish. I rigged Jessica up for anything that would bite, and she got right to it. Before I could get my own line in the water, she had already caught a couple of nice crappie and was already making plans to take them home to cook up for supper. We were having a wonderful experience—fishing, talking about life, and just enjoying the beauty of the outdoors.

Having passed some raspberry bushes on the trek in, we took some time to go back and pick a few; they were delicious.

As the afternoon progressed, I noticed some storm clouds gathering to the south. They were those beautiful clouds that blossom up with the heating of the afternoon and usually indicate an impending downpour of rain. The clouds continued to increase, and we continued to fill our stringer. Eventually hearing the thunder, I took a few moments to explain to Jessica the old Boy Scout technique of when you see the flash you can count 1,001, 1,002 . . . until you hear the thunder and know about how far away the lightning strike is. She was having a great time counting and informing me exactly how far away the lightening really was. I could tell as the counting got shorter, she was getting a little anxious. I suggested that we gather our things and head back to the truck. We decided to stop by and indulge in just a few more raspberries. While enjoying another round, a flash of lightning followed immediately by thunder got both our attentions. I looked to see the clouds' movement only to be interrupted by the mighty prayers of my six-year-old Jessica. She had thrown her fishing pole to the ground, and with eyes closed she was speaking boldly and frantically to God. Her words went something like this: "Dear God, please allow us to leave this place safely.

I know You can deliver us from the danger of this lightening—Amen." At this point she looked at me and said, "Daddy, it's time to go." I agreed, and we headed back to the truck. As I struggled to keep up with her, I kept thinking, Lord, she has it. I was both humbled and grateful.

What is your child's first response when she encounters a difficult or uncontrollable situation?

If she turns to God or if she comes to you for advice on how to turn to God, you're well on your way to seeing the training and the instruction of the Lord accomplished in her life.

Action Point: *Discover something that you and your daughter would love to do together. Make plans to do it. Include some time where you just set and talk.*

Chapter 2

"Everyone who calls upon the name of the
Lord shall be saved."

Romans 10:13

As a teaching pastor for over 17 years, I have preached about Salvation in Jesus Christ many times using many different illustrations and Scriptures. I almost always end up with Romans 10:13 when it comes time to respond. It was on a similar Sunday in 1999 that I had preached a message dealing with the subject of Salvation and man's need for Jesus that this next story takes place.

I must preface this story with a story from my own childhood. When I was growing up, my parents believed strongly that Sunday afternoon was a time for rest. After my brother and I got past the nap stage, our Sundays went something like this: church—lunch—outside, and don't come in unless you're bleeding or someone else is. My parents would rest. In particular my dad would sit in his recliner, turn on the TV, and soon sleep would subdue him. The only exception to this Sunday afternoon routine was during football season when my brother and I were allowed to watch the Dallas Cowboys with Dad. Well, we watched; Dad usually drifted off to sleep and would ask us later who won the game.

When I reached adulthood (which really only begins after you have children), I fully began to understand the routine that I had questioned as a young boy growing up; that is, after you have children, chase them around, change diapers and wipe them down after meals, you really could use a good nap. So Dayna and I developed a similar routine on Sunday afternoons: church—lunch—football—wake up and ask for the score. Usually I had to watch the late news/sports to find out this information because if Dayna hadn't gone to sleep, or if the girls realized I was asleep, they would turn the channel to some female-designed, estrogen-charged show. I might go to sleep watching the Cowboys and wake up watching *High School Musical*.

With that clarified let me turn your attention back to 1999. It was Sunday afternoon; church was finished, and Dayna had fed us all well. That means if the belly is full, the body needs rest. I sat down in my recliner to watch the Colts game on TV. Remember I am in Indiana, where you don't get the Cowboys much, and Peyton Manning has replaced basketball as the number-one Sunday afternoon pastime. It was cold out, so the girls were asked to play in their rooms while Mom and Dad rested. They did well, I guess, because I drifted off quickly. I grew restless at some point and had that uneasy feeling you get as a parent that your child is in need of you. I opened my eyes to find Jessica standing next to my chair staring at me. I love my daughters, but every time I wake up and they are staring at me, it always sort of messes with my mind just a bit. You know, it's two o'clock in the morning, and you awaken to find your child standing next to your bed just looking at you. So I ask her, "How you doing?"

She replies, "Fine."

I ask her, "So what's up?"

"Well," she says, "I have something I need to talk to you about."

I'm thinking okay what's broke, and or where's your sister? Little did I know that Jessica had been doing some serious thinking while I was watching or really dreaming about football.

She began, "Daddy, I've been thinking about Jesus."

I asked, "What were you thinking, Jessica?"

"Well, I heard you talking this morning about sin and our need for a Savior and I realized something. I don't always do the right thing, and I get in trouble, and I was thinking that Jesus could forgive me."

I quickly moved into pastor/dad role thinking I needed to clarify what my daughter was thinking about. I was just about to jump into a six-year-old's version of a Gospel presentation when Jessica simply announced to me, "While you were resting, I was lying on my bed talking to Jesus. Daddy, I asked Him to be my Savior and the Leader of my life." I began to cry; Jessica looked at me like what's up with this? I quickly informed her as her daddy I was just very proud and elated she had given her life to Jesus.

We never know as parents when the Spirit of God will speak to our children, and we should always pray that when He does, they are capable of listening to the call.

Have you talked to your children lately about lis-tening to the voice of God?

Action Point: *If you're not already praying for your child's salvation, make it a point to begin to do so. Talk with often about Jesus and how much He loves them.*

Chapter 3

"... a crushed spirit dries up the bones."
Proverbs 17:22

Our second daughter was having some learning difficulties. My first thought was she needed to memorize everything, and she would be okay. Dayna, a former educator, quickly noted I should know the rote system is not the answer to all learning problems. What the answer was in this situation was high-dollar testing. I reluctantly consented; the tests were done, and after waiting a few weeks for the results, I went into this meeting thinking I was going to observe some goofy philosophy on education and, of course, how much it would cost me. I was pleasantly surprised to hear the words, "Your daughter's I.Q. is off the chart;" followed by, "she is, however, dyslexic."

So I said, "That explains the letters turned around. What do we do about it?"

"Well, she needs to learn how to transfer information from one side of the brain to the other."

I reasoned this out, "She can walk and talk at the same time and even chew gum; what does this mean?"

"It's not quite that simple," replied the teacher. "Your daughter, for example, would be a person who is both left- and right-eye dominant."

"Great Scott!" I replied. "She can switch hit."

Both the teacher and my wife looked at me with, well, it was a look highly charged with estrogen. I grew quiet, and as the teacher continued talking with my wife, I'm thinking how do I begin to teach her to switch hit? I drifted off into a daydream about what an outstanding softball player she would become. By the way, last summer batting right handed, she hit .750 in her summer league and has a cannon for an arm—oops, a proud Dad moment.

Mikayla is just a fun kid to be around. She never stops making me proud, and she always seems to be a few steps ahead of her age group. What I mean is she is 12 going on 21. Every time a Mustang advertisement comes out in the paper, she is quick to point it out to me. I am also a Mustang fan but realize that every 16-year-old needs to start out in cars with dents so the ones they add won't really matter. When I point this out, she usually gives me that current young person phrase, "Whatever."

Mikayla has made tremendous advances in her academics, and for that Dayna and I are both grateful. I never cease to be amazed that even the most gifted among people struggle with issues whether naturally occurring or manmade. The key I have found with my daughters is to find out their niche—what makes them click—so to speak.

If you know your children well enough, and it requires some serious effort as a parent, the Lord will show you what it is that drives them. After all, He created them and wants them to discover that purpose.

How encouraging are you as your children develop through adversity?

Action Point: *Have you discovered what drives your daughter? Here's a hint. It will change somewhat as she grows and matures.*

Take time to get away and talk with your daughter about adversity and be sure to include sharing with her that the word of God is His gift to us to help equip us for adversity.

Chapter 4

"It is for freedom that Christ has
set us free."

Galatians 5:1

A few years ago I had the opportunity to go to Mexico on a mission trip. As I prayed about it, the Lord really impressed upon me that I should take my two oldest daughters with me. I was a little hesitant at first. I knew that where we were going was pretty safe, yet as a father I had reservations about taking two of my precious children outside the United States. I continued to pray, and God confirmed that I was supposed to take them with me. I informed them about how God was leading me and asked them to pray about it with me. They were excited to say the least, but I wanted them to understand the importance of God confirming in our hearts just how He wants to use us. After a few days of prayer, they came to the conclusion that they were indeed supposed to join Dad on the mission trip. We prepared letters together and sent these to many of our closest friends and family and asked them to help support us in our efforts. Specifically our request was they join us in prayer for our ministry to the Mexican people and for safety going and coming and finally in prayer for the financial support needed to make the trip. After praying over the letters, we mailed them out.

A couple of weeks later we began to receive some replies to our letters. Many responded they would pray for us while we ministered; others sent checks to help financially. Every day the same question would come up, "Have you been to the mail box yet?" And just about every day the Lord would encourage all of us with a note or financial gift. It was incredible to watch how my girls began to see that trusting God frees us up to do exactly what He calls us to do.

The day after Christmas we left for Mexico. The weather in Oklahoma was bitterly cold, but upon arriving in southwest Texas, the team discovered 70's and palm trees. The girls, the entire team, and I were elated. We took some time to go to the beach at South Padre Island the first day, which was the first time Jessica and Mikayla had seen the gulf. The water was cold, but it didn't stop them or many others from Oklahoma from getting wet.

The next day we headed into Mexico, and to be honest I was still a little hesitant—that father thing. The girls quickly jumped in with both feet and were excited to help any way they could. We visited door to door asking folks to come out to a special meeting, and over 150 showed up. After sharing Christ with them, many people gave their hearts to Jesus. We invited all who were there to a big festival that was being held at a local soccer field the following day.

Excited and anticipatory of what the next day held, the team returned to the hotel.

Early the next day people began arriving at the soccer field, and we each went to our assigned areas to work and share the Gospel. Every 45 minutes we rotated from one area to another to relieve other short-term missionaries. While all these different ministry areas were going on, many of the pastors and lay people were preaching from several platforms, and others were preparing to feed over 8,000 people.

I had the privilege to preach to several hundred people that day and to see many of them give their hearts to Christ. Our team was about to rotate to the neighborhood door-to-door time when I was asked to preach again. Just as I was about to ask some team members to keep and eye on the girls, something in my spirit said, "No, you should go with the team." Thankfully, I listened. A few minutes later we're going door to door inviting and sharing when one little girl came out into the yard to greet us. I asked her name and age, and she responded. I was just about to share with her about Christ when the Spirit said, "No." I thought to myself am I hearing God right? After all isn't this what we came to do? Just at that time Mikayla came up behind me and begin to visit with the girl through our interpreter. The Spirit said, "Mikayla is to share her faith."

I asked Mikayla to ask her if she would like to know how to receive Christ as her Savior. Mikayla asked with the interpreter's help, and when the girl said yes Mikayla just looked at me and said "Dad, how do I tell her?" I helped the interpreter, and before long we were to the point of praying with this little girl. As Mikayla led, the little girl prayed to receive Christ. At this point Dad became a blubbering giant. Jessica and Mikayla were looking at me and, I'm sure, wondering what's up with this. After a minute I was able to share with them how special it was for me to see one of my daughters lead someone to faith in Christ and how as a dad I knew someday Mikayla would be joined in eternity by this little girl, Norma. I was further able to explain that because we had accepted God's invitation to go, He had rewarded all of us with the joy of knowing we were following His will. Jessica and Mikayla came home from Mexico with a new appreciation for the country we live in and a heart for missions.

What are you doing to prepare your children for the calling of the freedom that Christ has called us all to proclaim?

Action Point: *Missions are a part of the calling that God has placed on every Christian. You don't have to leave the U.S. to do a mission project with your daughter, start in your community or somewhere nearby. Every child though needs to experience the high calling of God.*

Chapter 5

"Everyone should be quick to listen. . . ."

James 1:19

I love the outdoors, and my daughters do as well. On one particular occasion I was taking Lydia deer hunting with me. She was five at the time, and my nickname for her is Scooter. She never just walked; she always scooted her feet. In the woods where quiet is fairly important, her nickname is The Armadillo. If you've never seen one, it looks like an oversize rodent with body armor. This is not why she has the nickname, however. An armadillo makes its way along the forest floor looking for grubs and such to eat while making an incredible amount of noise.

Lydia does a great imitation of one any time we go hunting.

On this particular hunt I had planned, I was taking her to a spot where I had been seeing deer activity. I really wanted for her to see some deer up close and personal so she might catch the fever of the outdoors so to speak. Since Lydia is my third daughter, she has the advantage of Dad having made several mistakes with her older sisters. This means when we ventured out that day, I was better prepared for whatever might come up. I had plenty of food, drink, and of course, a staple for any father with daughters in the great outdoors, toilet paper.

We arrived at the stand about 3:30 in the afternoon, got settled, and I began to go over the essentials for seeing animals. One must remain very quiet and still. I know you're thinking five-years-old—yeah right. Well, she did great till the prime time of the evening—just before dark. I had run out of food, and she had to go to the bathroom. I had a coffee can just for this occasion, but then she got cold. I was getting a bit frustrated at this point, but she climbed up on my lap and snuggled close. I thought we're ready now; however, I didn't anticipate the every-30-second question, "Where are the deer?" This, of course, was audible not whispered—I am talking about The Armadillo.

So I scolded her, "We won't see anything if you don't hush." (I may have done this more than once.) I know this because I looked down at her after a longer-than-normal period of silence, and she was crying. I thought to myself, dear God, why did I bring this child to the woods? She seems to be so miserable.

God heard that prayer, and no sooner than I had thought it, His Spirit spoke to mine, "Rick, you're the one miserable. Your child just wants time with her father." Realizing what a dufus I had been, I apologized to Lydia and told her we could visit as much as she wanted to. Her face lit up, and we ended up enjoying the evening together.

Over the years I have realized that often my expectations will get in the way of an experience with my girls. I have learned to listen much more carefully and would recommend this discipline to any aspiring parent.

Let me ask you—are you truly listening to your child? Try listening not with the idea of just giving her an answer, but rather with an attitude that the only thing in the world that matters to you right now is listening to her. Isn't that the way God listens to us?

Action Point: Listening to your daughter is a learned behavior. Take some time this week to begin to develop the art of listening to your daughter. Here's a hint dad, they don't usually speak directly to any given subject. You must learn to listen and pry into their thought process so that you might listen more clearly.

Chapter 6

"... rather, serve one another in love."
Galatians 5:13

I often wonder what it would be like to travel abroad more often. I've been out of the country on several trips to Mexico and one ten-day trip to Nicaragua, but I would really like to see the world. All of my girls, except the twins, have been to Mexico with me. On one such trip into Mexico, I had all three of my oldest girls. Lydia was only six, so I was going to keep a very close eye on her and get some daddy-daughter time with her. Dayna was doing the same with the older two. Lydia had a blast. We went throughout the neighborhoods in Matamoris, and every house we came across she would say,

"Hola; co'mo esta?" ("Hi, how are you?") She was meeting more people than most of the adults and handing out tracts with the salvation message. We had a great time that day just enjoying being Jesus's mouthpiece.

Back at the hotel we all had group time, and Lydia, all six-years-old, shared how she had given out the tracts and met so many people; however, she was confused as to why so many people wanted to touch her head. (She has blond hair.) I explained it was a good-luck cultural thing. She was fine with this and looked forward to feeding and ministering to the many people the following day.

The next morning we arrived early in the area that was set up to feed approximately 8,000 people and began what would be a very full day. I explained to Lydia there would be a lot of people, and she needed to stay very close to Daddy. She said she understood and would be by my side at all times. As I would preach on the stages that were set up, little Lydia was right by my side. When I wasn't preaching, we would be working in different areas by playing games with the children and cooking and singing. Since Lydia loves to sing, she really enjoyed learning to sing in Spanish. About 3:00 P.M. we began the feeding lines, and that's when things got interesting.

As there were literally thousands of Mexican people in the lines, Lydia was finding it a little difficult to stay close to me. I was able to encourage some others to take our place in the line, and Lydia and I stepped out to pursue other opportunities. The only problem was every thing else had pretty much shut down in order to have enough people to serve the food. I asked Lydia what she thought we should do. She pondered for a minute and said first she needed a potty break. After we had walked all the way across the field and used the facilities, she said, "Dad, I know what we need to do."

I asked, "What?"

"We need to clean the trash up off this field and leave it looking nice for the Mexican people." I agreed and we went in search of trash bags.

We had so much fun picking up trash and putting it on the fire. I took several pictures of her as well as the other people from our group that joined in. When we left, she looked over that field and said, "Daddy, it just looks better."

I once read that someone asked a pastor in a remote country what he thought of Dawson Trotman, founder of The Navigators ministries. He replied, "Mr. Trotman cleaned the mud from my shoes." Our children can be fine examples of Christ by simply serving other people.

Have you asked your children to be involved in sharing their faith by serving?

Action Point: *Jesus calls us to serve our fellow man in love. You don't have to take a trip to a local soup kitchen or other service organization to serve. Simply look around your neighborhood and see if there is an elderly person you can do something special for and serve them with your daughter.*

Chapter 7

"Surprise, surprise, surprise!"

Gomer Pyle

"**T**wo are better than one," a wise man once wrote. I had my doubts about this when my wife showed up about a week before Christmas with a picture of a sonogram. I had seen these before—you know the protoplasm looking critter that is your child. I looked and thought to myself we weren't planning this, but God knows what He is doing. She asked me to look again as if I had added an OBGYN degree to my collection. I did as she asked, and still it didn't sink in. A good woman is priceless, and Dayna, holding my head as I looked for the third time, pointed out there were two pups on the sonogram photo. To say I instantly was aston-ished would be like saying the Eiffel Tower is a big radio antenna. I quickly gathered myself and asked if there could be a mistake. I mean, you know, med-icine is not a hundred-percent science, and well, I needed a second opinion.

Dayna assured me it was no mistake, and if all went well, we would be adding two additions. Okay, I thought, 50/50 odds of a male child, but if you read the introduction, you know God's design is what I like to call the Harrison tribe of women. I might add here that God indeed knows what He is doing because if He had blessed us with the twins first, we probably would have thought that's all the blessing we can take.

As I write this chapter, the twins are seven-years-old and going strong. They, just like all my other daughters, love time with their daddy. I have found it is much easier to get to know them one-on-one rather than together. I tried taking both of them fishing last spring, and let's just say it resembled something only *chaos* would begin to come close to describing. It was a great day outdoors, but very little bonding took place unless you can count removing a fish hook from the back of my hand as a good situation. They both watched and squirmed as I carefully and surgically cut the hook from my hand. The rest of the afternoon I devoted to teaching them both how to go to the bathroom outdoors. This is very essential for every child to learn and should not be attempted except by a professional dad.

Two things I have noted about my twin daughters. First, they are as different as night and day. Secondly and more importantly, they both have a great longing to be independent. Sure, they can communicate almost telepathically at times, but like all children they long to impress those around them with their ability to do it on their own. I have also discovered with my other daughters this can be a positive attribute if channeled in the right direction. I would encourage you to investigate this area with your child. Some parents want their child to be completely independent which sounds good on paper. I would rather my children understand how to be independently dependent upon their Heavenly Father. In Hebrews 11:6 the Scripture tells us, "Without faith it is impossible to please God, for he that comes to God must believe that He rewards those that diligently seek Him." In other words, if we believe God loves us, provides for us, cares about everything that goes on in our lives, shouldn't we want to depend upon Him in every area of our lives?

Do your children understand the meaning of faith, and have you determined to model faith for your children as they mature into adulthood?

Action Point: *It is never too early to ask your child how to determine God's will. The reason being, that you want to guide them in this discovery process of how God speaks to us. My twins are now almost 8 and we discuss these thoughts on our adventures outdoors. Take a trip with your daughter to some-*

where she enjoys going and teach here about dis-covering God's will.

Chapter 8

"So we fix our eyes not on what is seen,
but on what is unseen. For what is
seen is temporary, but what is
unseen is eternal."

2 Corinthians 4:18

I have a photograph in my office that means more to me than the actual picture. The picture itself is a beautiful fall afternoon with the sun shining as it sets across trees, highlighting the fall colors, as if God Himself painted it. Although quite pleasant to look at, the picture does nothing to describe what it means to me. You see, the real meaning of the picture is found on the back. There you will find the words written to me from my oldest daughter, Jessica. She even says she isn't sure when or where she took the picture. What really matters is I have the time to take her with me into the great outdoors. She tells me she cherishes those times. The cool thing is so do I. I would rather spend an afternoon with one of my girls in the beauty of the outdoors talking about life or whatever else they might have on their minds. The other cool thing is they know it.

On another wall, actually a divider of one of my bookcases, is where I display all the artwork that has been given to me by my younger ones. They are reminders to me that I have only so much time to influence them on this planet. They also remind me of how much they enjoy showing love towards their daddy. I wish I took the more time than I do to show my appreciation to my Heavenly Daddy. I'm convinced one way we do this is by showing our children how much we appreciate what they mean to our lives. I am further convinced this kind of love must be tangible. God teaches us love is not something we hide under a basket, but rather it is something we express to others in works of service.

I have found when it comes to building strong relationships with my daughters I have to put a lot into it. I'm talking about thinking, planning, and even committing to time blocks that will allow me to develop the quality relationships that will endure. I know this: when I received that photograph from Jessica I couldn't fight back the tears; my daughter had made me feel genuinely loved.

<u>Are your children convinced that your time with them is not a burden</u>?

Dads, I believe we set an example of God by giving our children quality, genuine time.

Action Point: *What is your daughter's favorite thing to do? It is a hint to their love language. I would encourage you to take all the time necessary to discover here language and use it to speak to her. God created it in her and she not only needs to discover it, she also needs to know how to use it.*

Chapter 9

"... perfect love drives out fear. ..."

1 John 4:18

I finally got smart recently. The twins had been asking me to take them hunting for some time, and I knew from past experience tree stands just weren't workable with little ones. I decided to build a blind that could be set up on the ground. The girls could move around in it without being as easily noticed, and the sounds they would make wouldn't be as easily heard by the animals we were hunting. Since the girls in particular love to deer hunt, I got a plan on paper, bought the lumber, and decided to take Samantha with me to participate in the building of this blind. She readily agreed, and we set off for the outdoors.

Upon arriving I dressed her in the necessary boots to keep the stickers to a minimum and tucked her pants in her boots. Unfortunately, I couldn't tuck her hands and hair and everything else into the boots. Later I spent about 30 minutes and half a pint of blood getting all the stickers out. I quickly decided that Samantha should be moved into management, and she could best oversee this project from the back of the truck. Once I got everything set up, I began to assemble the blind which to Samantha looked like a doll house. She kept asking when the "doll house" would be completed and if we could go get sissies to play in the "doll house."

I explained that this was actually a hunting blind, and we would paint it together as soon as daddy got all the pieces assembled. She wanted to know why we weren't seeing any deer if this was a hunting blind. Okay, by now I was ready to fire the management, but wanting to be patient, I just ignored several questions that I couldn't possibly answer in a loving sort of manner. Twenty minutes later and a couple hundred questions later the blind was ready to be painted. Samantha had a great time helping to spray the paint on the blind and herself and me. It was fun, well at least until we heard the tiritos. Tiritos, also known as coyotes in the American heartland, had begun to stir not far from where we had set up the blind.

When they begin to move in the evening shortly before dusk, they howl and carry on loudly, and Samantha was convinced those tiritos were coming to get us. She clung to my leg like it was a safety post. I tried to talk her through her fear but to little avail. Even though she was securely holding on to Daddy, the fear was still there. I decided to experiment. I asked Samantha if she believed Daddy could run those coyotes off; she shook her head no. I asked her if I could try; she shook her head yes. I walked over to the edge of the field with a daughter wrapped to my leg and yelled at the coyotes, "Go away and don't come back." Samantha looked at me like is that the best you got? I started walking back to the truck, and they let loose again. This time in my best angry voice, I yelled, "Go on; get out of here, or I'm coming over there to get you." Samantha didn't care for this option and let me know it. I suggested that my last yell had put the fear of Daddy into those tiritos, and she could bet on it, so let's finish painting. She hesitantly let go of my leg and sprayed a few times and then informed me she would like to finish waiting in the truck. I obliged her, and we both waited there with the windows rolled down and listened for any more signs of the coyotes.

Finally, at almost dark she said, "Daddy, I think you scared them good that last time." I hope in time she will begin to realize that fear will always get in the way of love, and that real love will always neutralize fear.

All children struggle with their share of fears.

How will you prepare them to handle real or imagined fears as they approach adulthood?

Action Point: *Whether you're outdoors around some coyotes, white water rafting or riding a roller coaster, all can evoke fear in the heart of your daughter. I would encourage you to take your daughter to the limits of their fear. All the while, standing beside her – just like God stands beside us.*

Chapter 10

"... be strong in the grace that is
in Christ Jesus."

2 Timothy 2:1

So you are making your way through parent-hood, and what happens next? Your children become teenagers. I know many reading this book were wondering when I was going to get to this chapter. I now have one that is 17, and a second who will soon be 16. I swear on all that is holy that hor-mones, aliens, or brain damage occurred somewhere in the midst of a two-year period. I only know one way to combat this ongoing experiment—GRACE. If it were not for the grace of God and a very calm wife and mother, I believe we would have already had our oldest daughter committed to either NASA or a state agency.

Jessica, whom I have talked about before, has always loved to fish with her daddy. This past summer I called and asked her, "Would you like to go fishing this afternoon?"

There was a long pause before she replied, "Yeah, I guess so." I wasn't real sure how to interpret this, so I told her we were going to a honey hole of a spot. In about an hour I picked her up. On the way we were able to visit about life, and as I asked her questions about this or that, she expressed herself with, "I guess so" or "I don't know."

We did have a lengthy conversation about how "lame" my radio station was. My mind wandered back about 35 years to a similar conversation I had had with my dad. His response was something like, "You don't know what good music is."

Eventually we arrived at the pond to fish, and Jessica helped me unload the boat. Actually she watched and asked if her feet had to get wet. I did my best to assure her they wouldn't and then waded up to my knees to insure this. At last the boat was launched, and we were fishing. Well, to be exact, I was fishing; Jessica was lathering up with sun screen or sun enhancer. I don't know for sure what it was except it smelled like a beach with a lot of coconuts. I handed her a pole with a special bait I had tied on guaranteed to catch big bass. She made a couple of casts and then placed the pole across her lap and applied some more sun stuff. I was watching in disbelief as she rolled up her sleeves and took off her socks and shoes and just lay back and took in the rays. I, on the other hand, was doing what we were created to do—FISH.

I asked if she planned on fishing today. She replied, "I just want to work on my tan." She added that it was okay for me to fish if I wanted to. This was the same daughter from chapters before who would beg me to take her fishing. I was now relegated to captain of a pond-hopping suntan cruiser. I had to laugh at this point because figuring out your teenager is like trying to fly a kite in a hurricane. You had better be prepared for the unpredictable, or your kite (child) will take off without you. Because God is gracious and because I need to be as well, Jessica and I had a fun afternoon, and I was able to razz her pretty good about it.

<u>How are you at displaying grace to your children</u>?

Godly GRACE loves us despite our quirks, changes, disappointments, or even our brain damage. I hope that all my girls recover by the time they're about 23.

Action Point: *Do you have a good enough relationship with your daughter(s) to have fun and tease a little in the midst of the changes they will or are going through. If your answer is no, commit to do whatever is necessary to establish this kind of relationship.*

Chapter 11

"There's no crying in baseball."

Tom Hanks
from *A League of Their Own*

As I mentioned earlier, I am an ex-football coach. I have had many enjoyable moments watching young men accomplish extraordinary things on the football field, in the classroom, and in their lives. It should come to no one's surprise except mine that little girls don't respond to the same sort of stimuli that young men do.

A great example of this was the first year I spent coaching my two oldest girls' softball team. I spent the first month perplexed most of the time. When I wasn't perplexed, I was confused. Apparently little girls don't follow softball to the same extent that little boys follow baseball. Some of this would include knowing what a ball and strike count are or what turning a double play means. I purposely moved Mikayla up to play on Jessica's team so I wouldn't have to chase two teams, and Mikayla was a bit ahead of her class talent wise.

It started out slow, kind of like remedial softball for girls. I taught them how to catch a ball, hold the bat, slide into a base, and where to stand in the batter's box. With all that training you would think they were ready for the ten-and-under league. But remember we are talking about girls here. I am not a chauvinist by any stretch of the imagination, but it doesn't take a rocket scientist to figure out there is a difference between boys and girls.

We did well the first inning, and the score was five to three our team. The next inning the opponent scored seven runs and that was because the league only allowed no more than seven runs per inning. Somewhere in the midst of our 16 errors for the inning, I said something—in my football coach's voice—like, "Girls, let's pay attention to what we're doing on the field."

As the girls made their way back to the dugout at the end of the scoring spree, I noticed three of them crying. I asked them if they were hurt, and they simply shrugged their shoulders. I tried to pursue it only to get some advice from my assistant coach, who was the mother of one of the girls. She said, "They're just girls, Rick."

I'm a little slow, being a guy and all, so I asked her what that meant. She replied, "You scared them." I felt terrible but still didn't know what that meant. I thought to myself I didn't demean or single out anyone. How did I scare them?

So I asked Mikayla and Jessica, "Did Daddy scare you?

They simply replied, "No, Daddy, we are used to you being loud." (They had attended many football practices.) I decided no more loud until I met with the girls and explained it was nothing personal, and I only wanted to be sure to get their attention.

Later that evening I thought back on this and remembered Tom Hanks's character from *A League of Their Own* and his infamous statement: "Cry? There's no crying in baseball." Like Hanks did in the movie, I've learned that little women's feelings are very important to them. I still continue to coach softball and haven't had any crying in a long time.

How sensitive are you to your little girl's emotions and the condition of her heart?

Isn't it important that we clarify how and why we speak the way we do?

Action Point: *Dad if you're not quick to apologize and ask forgiveness when you aren't sensitive to your daughters emotional needs – commit to become this way. I know from experience that our daugh-*

ters need a dad who is sensitive to their sometimes fragile emotions.

Chapter 12

"How many go's-n-ta's?"

Jethro Bodine

Have you ever wondered how much money it takes to make ends meet in a large family? Well, let me first say more than you would imagine; secondly, God provides outstandingly. I was recently discussing this with my wife. Actually the subject was over my tribe of women's twenty-dollar-a-week toilet paper habit combined with the number of hair-care products necessary to accommodate this same tribe. I mean when you get in the shower and you're middle aged and balding, you just need a bar of soap, And if you use shampoo, it doesn't really matter if it holds and lifts. Just give me the simple brand.

If you are a member of the Harrison tribe of women, you individually have all the toiletries. I can't and don't wish to keep up with this; however, I know it continues to get more expensive. So I decided as an experiment with my tribe, I would calculate their number of toiletries verses my number of deer blinds, rifle shells and fishing lures. I thought for sure that I would come out smelling like a rose. What I didn't count on was new math. I learned math at the Jethro Bodine School of math; you know, how many goes into that. I honestly thought math was simple. My wife explained it to me like this, "Rick, the girls each have their individual needs." I nodded. This is my way of reaching a conclusion with my wife when I really have no idea what she is talking about.

What I learned was basically I could retire when I'm 120 years old, or I could invest in both a toilet paper and a cosmetic manufacturing company and retire at 60. I decided to go with the investment plan. The only problem I foresee is that after buying all this stuff, I don't have any investment capital left over; well, unless you count investing in shotguns, rifles or the newest rod-and-reel combo.

Seriously, if you were to get caught up in how much your family costs, you would have a break down. I know in my case God has used my family to show me how He can show Himself. Many times we have simply prayed as a family for a genuine need only to see God provide in a miraculous way. Someone has coined the phrase, "God is good all the time; all the time God is good." I firmly believe this. Never let finances get in the way of family.

How can you include your children in the process of praying for needs?

Even if it is going to take a miracle, have you included your children in this process? Remember—before you know it, they are going to be in your place. They need an example.

Action Point: *It may sound overly simplistic but, you're daughter will soon be 18 and out of the house. She needs to know how to intercede to her heavenly Father for her needs. Let me encourage you to include your daughter(s) in prayer time for specific family needs. Include her in the answers to these prayers.*

Chapter 13

"Mighty Warrior"

I don't know if you've ever thought of your daughter as a mighty warrior or not. I do know one thing I want my daughters to understand is they can accomplish incredible things by the power of God. I don't want them to think they are capable of anything they set their minds to. Rather, I want them to understand what God calls us to do He not only equips us with the necessary talents, but often times He simply wants to show us His glory. His ability to accomplish things through humans is legendary, and the Bible is full of these stories not as stories to read but as examples of God's kindness to those who follow Him with all that they have. One of my favorite stories is of Gideon in the book of Judges. He is a guy hiding out trying to get enough grain together to make a loaf of bread when the angel of God appears to him and renames him.

You see in God's eyes we are as He created us to be, and there are no limitations. Often times what happens to us is life's experiences will allow the enemy to creep in and limit what we believe can occur. Mainly this is based on experiences and not on God's Word. God's Word teaches us that nothing is impossible with Him.

With this in mind I recently took Lydia on a hunting trip where we talked about life and the future. Lydia is a cool kid and has all kinds of potential; however, she has lacked confidence in herself in the past partly because of her age and partly because of her birth order. She went from being the baby of the family to Lydia in the middle. As we are talking about this in the deer blind, Lydia asks, "How do you know when you understand what God has called you to do?" I explained that the key is getting to know God, and we do this by spending time in God's Word and by simply talking with God and asking the Holy Spirit to guide us to understand what His will is. I explained to her that one way to know you are involved in doing what God wants you to do is you know that the end results rest solely in His hands and not in our abilities. I told her the story of Gideon, and we talked about how he must have felt and the real fears he must have faced.

It was a very profitable afternoon, and as we talked about the future, she shared with me about reading how a young girl her age had killed a hog and deer in the same weekend. She thought it would be fun to be involved in the harvesting of a deer or other animal, and I agreed. That afternoon we made plans to go to a hunter safety education course the next spring, and we would also spend more time learning to shoot. She was elated, especially after I was able to harvest a nice deer later in the day. I was so proud of her as we approached the animal, and she quickly opened its mouth to inspect the teeth to see how old it was. She gave me a high five and told me she had had a blast.

One thing I have learned in trying to prepare my children for the future and their understanding of God is that what we often think will go over their heads really will not.

Lydia is only eleven as of this writing, but she is intrigued about spiritual things because we take the time to talk about them.

How much time are you investing to ensure your children understand who they are in the Lord Jesus?

Action Point: *Plan a weekend away with your daughter. It really doesn't matter where you go — simply go have fun and take along your bible and something for both of you to journal in. At the end of the weekend share with each other what God shard with you from His Word.*

Chapter 14

"You're my one and only friend."
SpongeBob SquarePants

Emma and Samantha are unique. Not only are they twins they are, most of the time, best friends. It is interesting to listen in on their conversations. One day Emma is Mom and Samantha is Dad. Next day they switch. From time to time they are even each other's pet. Occasionally they both will come up to me and let me know that I am their best daddy. It makes me feel warm and fuzzy inside even though I know that they are only seven.

On the other hand, I think sometimes we would honor God if we spoke with Him, "You're my best Daddy!" as the twins speak to their earthly father.

One day the twins and I decided to go to the park. They really enjoy sliding and swinging and jumping with each other. They also expect Dad to be just as big a kid as they. On this particular occasion they had decided that Dad should go down the barrel slide with them. I must confess I was a college athlete and played summer ball up into my mid-thirties; however, I am now rather robust around the waistline. I once had a friend who told me to be careful as you age; your brain will get your body into very dangerous situations. Well, this was one of those occasions. The twins asked and I couldn't resist.

Samantha went first and then Emma; then it was my time. I decided to go head first; I mean, I used to do it that way. The slide was slippery and away I went. Down, down, down I descended, and then the wedge took place. I was hung up in the barrel and pointed downhill. You know as well as I do that means blood rushing to the head and so on. The twins were elated that Dad had produced a new trick. They were completely amused. I wasn't.

I decided to act on my situation with that Boy Scout mentality of don't panic, access the situation, and make a plan. My plan was to do my best to roll over and pull myself up the slide and do all this before I passed out. Emma and Samantha noticed that perhaps this wasn't a trick and began to do what little girls do—ask questions.

I don't know about you, but when I am upside down in a barrel with my head as red as a tomato, I am not really in the mood to answer questions about how come my face is so red. I was able to get my arms in position to pull myself out when I realized the twins had climbed back up the slide to help. Emma was actually on top pulling my shoes off, and Samantha was on my shoulders, hanging on, making sure she didn't slide down the slide. When it was all done, I had pulled myself out of the barrel with Samantha holding my shirt over my head, and I was barefoot. I righted myself and decided that the swings were better suited to the time we had left. At the end of the day, Sam and Emma both hugged me, kissed me, and told me I was their best daddy.

Are you teaching your girls about fun?

I know Jesus was fun to be around. Shouldn't we as parents show that to our children?

Action Point: *What does your daughter(s) like to do for fun? Whatever it is take some time and go with them and be silly and have fun.*

Chapter 15

"Without faith it is impossible to
please God. . . ."

Hebrews 11:6

I can't think of a more faith challenging experience than to teach your children to drive. I begin this process with my girls when they are thirteen. I know, yes, the driving age is 16 in most states, but when you are driving a country road or out in a wheat field, there just aren't a lot of traffic officers around. It's rather interesting; just like each child is different, so is her ability to comprehend driving.

With Jessica, my oldest, she began her driving practice on a stick shift. It took her a little bit of effort and some transmission shavings to get the hang of it, but mercy, did she light up when she finally got to second gear. Now that she is 17 and driving legally, we occasionally venture out to the country roads just to learn a little more and to enjoy a time of conversation. It was on one of these recent road trips I realized something about girls. They have the same depth perception that adult women do. I kid you not. A truck was fast approaching our truck from the other direction, and it was all I could do to keep Jessica from steering us into the bar ditch. I suggested that the road was wider than it appeared, but she was absolutely sure it was narrower. You may be saying that I'm a sexist, but I have proof. Not two days later Mikayla did the same thing. Mikayla further exhibits this behavior any time she is behind the wheel of a moving vehicle. As my faith is weak and the ditch is within reach out the window on my side of the truck, I find myself regularly reaching over to correct her steering. You heard me right. My faith is weak.

When I am in the passenger seat, I quickly realize that my two oldest girls are not that far away from leaving the road (I mean home). Not too far in the distant future, they will no longer be under my rules and regulations. They will no longer have to ask permission to go here or there. They will have the opportunity to be independent; however, I hope they choose to be dependent, not on me or their mother (We love them but look forward to the day they go to college or to work and come to visit and then go home.) but to be dependent on their Heavenly Father.

It's one of the things we talk about when we drive. What does God hold for your future?

How do you know when you know he's the right guy for you?

What makes our lives pleasing in God's sight?

<u>Do you promote faith conversations with your kids</u>?

It's never too early to start. They might surprise you with how much they long to know about trusting God.

Action Point: *Plan times with your daughter(s) where you discuss the big pictures in life. She needs your advice even if you are human and struggle with faith like every other dad.*

Chapter 16

"Goodnight and God Bless."
                                    Red Skelton

One of the most intriguing passages in the Bible is found in 1 John 3:1-2. God looks upon all of us as His children, and one of the most challenging tasks any parent has is to be a good example of how God treats His children. I find great comfort in knowing that I am God's child, adopted through Jesus Christ, and entitled to everything that Christ has given me. I want my children to understand that God holds nothing back from His children and loves them with an everlasting love that doesn't change based on their performance or lack thereof. I also want them to know that as God's children they have special responsibilities to their fellow man and special privileges reserved for each and everyone of them who asks.

The risk that all of us face whether we are raising girls or boys or a mix is communicating love effectively, regularly, and honestly with our children. The only way I know to accomplish our goal is to spend a lot of time in God's Word and on our knees and with our Heavenly Daddy. I think the same is true in order to calculate success with our children. If when we look back someday and our children have developed a genuine love relationship with their Heavenly Daddy, I believe we've reached the goal set before us as parents.

One big key is don't take yourself nor your children too seriously.

Have fun, laugh at yourself, laugh with your wife, and laugh at each other.

<u>Now, laugh with your children</u>!

Action Point: *Learning to laugh at ourselves is a necessity for being a loving father. Never let your pride get in the way. (Have Fun!!!)*

Contact Info:
Rick Harrison
Mighty Warrior Ministries
858 Mimosa Dr.
Watonga, Ok 73772
(580) 623-5158
(580) 791-1876
www.mw-ministries.org

LaVergne, TN USA
06 April 2011
223186LV00001B/1/P